Season of the White Stork

Season of the
White Stork

by Heiderose and Andreas Fischer-Nagel

A Carolrhoda Nature Watch Book

Carolrhoda Books, Inc./Minneapolis

Editorial Consultant: Dr. Dwain W. Warner, Curator of Ornithology and Professor, The Bell Museum of Natural History, Minneapolis, MN

Photograph on page 44 by A. Cruickshank/VIREO

This edition first published 1986 by Carolrhoda Books, Inc.
Original edition published 1984 by Kinderbuchverlag Luzern AG, Lucerne, Switzerland, under the title DAS STORCHENJAHR © 1984
Translated from the German by Elise H. Scherer
Adapted by Carolrhoda Books, Inc.

Manufactured in the United States of America

LIBRARY OF CONGRESS CATALOGING IN PUBLICATION DATA

Fischer-Nagel, Heiderose.
  Season of the white stork.

  Translation of: Das Storchenjahr.
  "A Carolrhoda nature watch book."
  Summary: Describes the physical characteristics and behavior of the white stork as it reproduces and raises its young on rooftop nests throughout the spring and summer seasons.
  1. White stork—Behavior—Juvenile literature.
  2. White stork—Infancy—Juvenile literature.
  3. Parental behavior in animals—Juvenile literature.
  4. Birds—Behavior—Juvenile literature. 5. Birds—Infancy—Juvenile literature. [1. White stork.
  2. Storks] I. Fischer-Nagel, Andreas. II. Title.
  QL696.C535F5713 1986   598'.34   85-13274
  ISBN 0-87614-242-0 (lib. bdg.)

1 2 3 4 5 6 7 8 9 10 93 92 91 90 89 88 87 86

For our daughter Tamarica

INTRODUCTION

Most of us have heard the old myth that storks bring babies, but few of us know much about these beautiful birds. The white storks we recognize from fables and fairy tales are not found in North America, so many of us have never seen one. But for many years these storks have built their nests on the rooftops and chimneys of buildings throughout Europe, particularly in Germany, Holland, and Scandinavia. People thought the storks brought good luck and were always glad to welcome them back in the spring. Today people still look forward to the storks' return, but there are fewer and fewer storks to welcome.

The white stork has become rarer and rarer until today it is threatened with **extinction**. This has happened partly because there is less food for the stork. The marshy meadows that used to supply white storks with more than enough frogs to eat are now too dry to support the frog population. Power lines and factory smokestacks are also dangerous to the stork. They are often deadly obstacles to it in its flight. Like many other birds, the stork is a **migratory** bird. This means that it spends the summer in one climate and the winter in another. White storks spend their summers in Europe and their winters in Africa.

Heiderose and Andreas Fischer-Nagel live in Germany. When the German Federation for the Protection of Birds chose the white stork as the Bird of the Year for 1984, the Fischer-Nagels wanted to contribute to that effort. Over a long period of time they have observed different stork nests at close range and photographed the comings and goings of the stork families so that readers everywhere could become acquainted with these magnificent birds.

From the middle of March, when spring comes to Germany, the white storks begin to arrive from their winter homes in Africa. The male storks are almost always the first to return. After a long flight of over 6,000 miles (10,000 km), they usually land, sure of their targets, on the rooftop nests they left the autumn before. These nests are called **aeries**.

Storks are almost voiceless. They usually communicate by a clattering noise, made by clapping the two parts of their bills together. White storks make such a racket that they have been nicknamed "clatter storks." The male starts clattering almost as soon as he has landed. He is claiming his aerie and warning other male storks to keep away.

In a few days the female stork arrives. She looks just like the male, although slightly smaller. Often she will have been the male's mate the year before. The male greets her with vigorous clattering, and the female joins in.

Everyone in town knows from the noise that the storks have returned and spring has arrived.

The two birds patter excitedly around on the nest, flapping and clattering. If the female stork decides to stay with the

nest and the male, the pair will begin to carefully test and improve the future stork nursery. Some years the aerie becomes so big and heavy that in the autumn, after the birds have flown south again, people must make it smaller and prop it up. Otherwise the roofs of their houses could collapse. Some aeries have been known to weigh over 100 pounds (45 kg).

Both while they are nest building and later, the stork couple must be on the alert for other storks in the neighborhood. Storks are only too happy to steal another stork's nesting material, or even another stork's nest. Because of this, one of the storks usually stays on the nest while the other gathers material. If another stork attempts an attack anyway, the result can be a long battle on the aerie or in the air. If a battle happens after eggs have been laid, the eggs can fall out of the nest and break.

When the rough nest structure of sticks and stems is completed, the storks gather turf and grass, horse manure, hay, feathers, bits of cloth, and even plastic bags with which to line it. The birds adeptly work everything into the already existing nest or into the artificial base prepared for them by people. During this time they mate several times. To mate the male flies onto the back of the standing female and ejects his **sperm** into her. Only then can the female lay **fertilized eggs** in which little storks will develop.

As soon as the nest is ready, toward the end of April or the beginning of May, the female stork lays her first egg. The eggs are pure white, slightly shiny, and about as large as they are pictured here. Every two days the female lays another egg, two to five eggs altogether. After she has laid two eggs, the parents usually begin to **incubate** them. They sit down on the nest of eggs and keep them warm with their bodies.

Incubation lasts 33 days, a little over a month. During this time the male and female storks take turns sitting on the nest so that the nest is never unprotected and each adult has a chance to get food. Each time one returns to the nest, the two storks greet each other with enthusiastic clattering.

bird moves and stretches itself again and again. A tiny bill can be seen, then a foot and a wing. Then the little chick must rest again because hatching is tiring work. With its next attempt, this chick gets its head out of the egg.

After 33 days the first chick hatches. At first only a tiny hole can be seen in the eggshell. Slowly it gets bigger and the blunt end is lifted off by the chick inside. The little stork opens the egg-shell with its sharp **egg tooth**—a small, hard knob near the tip of the upper side of the chick's bill that will fall off a day or two after it hatches. The little

Worn out, the chick sinks onto the floor of the nest. Its head seems much too big for its thin neck, and its bill is not long and red like its parents' bills. The feathers on its head are completely wet. It's hard to imagine that this little heap will become a three-foot-tall stork one day.

Now the little stork begins to work with its strong legs. Little by little, it pushes its body out of the eggshell.

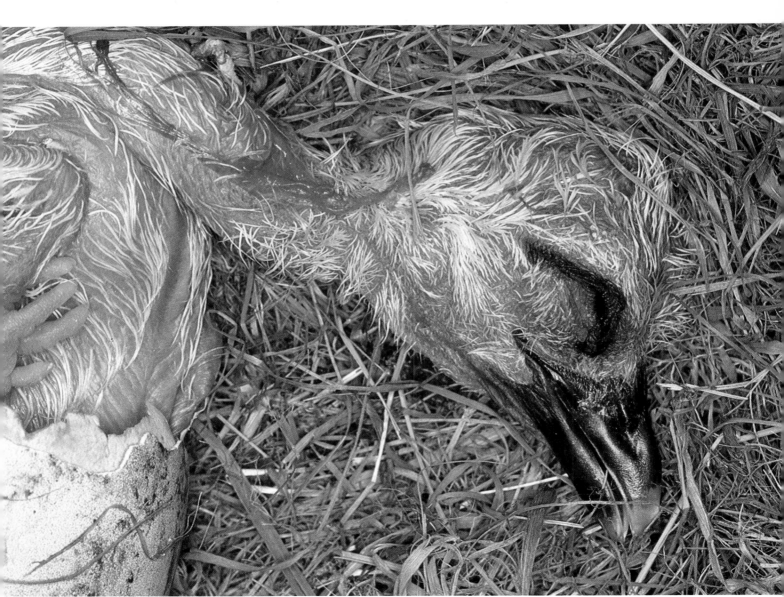

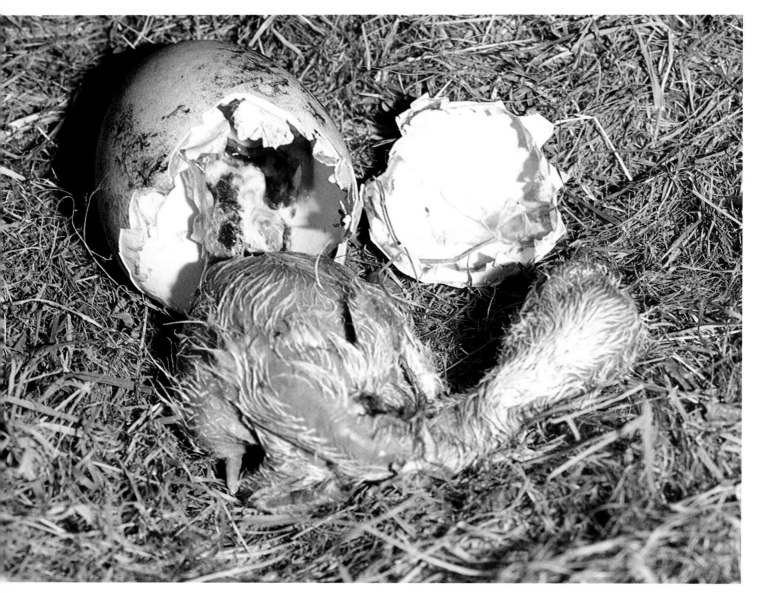

Finally the job is finished. The eggshell lies in two pieces, and the little stork lies nearby. Its body looks bulky and egg-shaped. At birth the chick weighs about 2 to 3 ounces (about 65 to 80 g), about the same as two chicken eggs. Its first fine down feathers are still matted together and its eyes are still closed, but they will open soon.

Now the parents begin to **brood**. Very

carefully, as if it were still the breakable egg, they sit over their newborn and keep it warm and dry.

Most of the remaining eggs will hatch at one-day intervals, but unfortunately not all the chicks will survive. Some will be too weak, or there may not be enough food for all of them.

After just one day, the chick already looks different. Its white down feathers have dried, and it can hold up its heavy head for a while. It's already hard to believe that the chick could have fit into its egg!

The next few days are very dangerous for the chick. Cold, wet weather can transform the nest into a deadly mud bath. If the sun shines too intensely, the chicks can be hurt from the heat. And there's often a crow around just waiting for an unguarded moment in which to seize a little stork. Because

of this, the parents keep watch constantly over the nest during the first few days, brooding and shading their young ones. Both parents will leave the aerie only after the chicks have grown and need more food.

While they are young, stork chicks can whine, croak, and whistle as well as clatter and, like young birds everywhere, they clamor for food. The parents feed them earthworms, beetles, grasshoppers, and other insects.

Although storks are popular, some people have made the birds' lives difficult. Where once there were meadows and brooks, today there are apartment complexes and dry, dusty fields. Storks can no longer find food in those places, and many stork babies die from lack of food. Only one or two young ones will survive to leave the aerie fully grown and healthy.

If the storks find an area as beautiful as the one in this picture, they will always have enough food: frogs, water beetles, fish, and much more. But even then the stork faces dangers. It's a long flight to Africa, and many storks crash into power lines or die from other causes on their way. Once they have reached Africa, they face the danger of being hunted and shot.

White storks catch and eat frogs, grasshoppers, mice, fish, and even snakes. They search for their food in marshy meadows. Very slowly the stork walks along, its head raised. Then suddenly it lunges at its prey, sometimes spreading its wings dramatically. The white stork's pointed, red bill is about 6 to 8 inches (15 to 20 cm) long.

Like many other birds, storks have **crops** in their necks. A crop is a kind of storage bag for food. A parent stork will fill its crop with food, then return to its hungry chicks and regurgitate, or bring up, the food for them to eat. If the stork has taken the food for its own use, it swallows the food from the crop farther down into its stomach.

A white stork looks alert and clever when it searches for food. Often it will suddenly stand still, hold one leg in the air a little, and lean its head to one side, listening. Suddenly it lunges. A good aim, the stork has probably captured something and gulped it down.

If it rains a lot, the stork chicks turn from white to dirty gray. They become completely covered with mud from the aerie floor. Then one of the parents will often sit with the delicate chicks in order to warm them and dry them.

While one parent is searching for food, the other uses its guard time to clean and smooth its feathers. This is called **preening**. Every single feather is pulled through the stork's bill, cleaned, and carefully poked back into its place. The stork uses its foot to clean those places its bill won't reach.

Because scientists are eager to know more about storks and prevent their extinction, they need a way to keep track of the birds after they have left the aeries. So while the chicks are still in the nest, a scientist from an ornithological station, a scientific institute for research on the life of birds, climbs up to the aerie and places a light metal ring around one leg of each chick. This is called **banding**. The name of the ornithological station and an identification number are printed on the ring. If the stork is observed, caught, or found dead after it leaves the aerie, people can notify the ornithological station. In this way scientists can investigate how far the stork flew, in which direction, and how quickly it made the trip.

Soon the little storks are strong enough to stand in the nest or, like two of the storks pictured above, sit on their elbows. They are also beginning to look like their parents. The parent birds can now leave the aerie for longer periods of time.

Before learning to fly, the storks must

exercise their wings. Over and over they stretch and spread their wings and carefully groom their feathers. Each stork has a gland above its tail that secretes an oil. When preening, the storks use their bills to spread this oil on their feathers to help keep them pliable and water resistant.

At the age of about two months, the great moment arrives. The young stork spreads its wings and attempts its first flight. The chick is now called a **fledgling**. This fledgling made it to the next chimney. Still a bit shaky, it stands on this unaccustomed slippery surface. Now and then the young storks fall from such a chimney, but they seldom hurt themselves. Helpful people set them back up on the roof, from which they will try again.

Because they do not want the white stork to disappear, bird lovers constantly watch the few remaining aeries and take the young storks out of the nest if they are in danger. They bring the birds to stork stations where they are examined, fed, and cared for.

Occasionally a parent dies during the incubation period. The remaining stork parent cannot incubate the eggs alone and later feed the young ones. It must leave the nest again and again to search for food, and during this time the eggs or the chicks are unprotected. When this happens, people intervene. The eggs are placed in an **incubator**, a special heated container for hatching eggs away from the parents, until they are ready to hatch.

Because young storks need a lot of attention, the rearing of a newly hatched stork is rather difficult for people. But stations for the care and rearing of young storks help us learn much more about them.

By August the last young stork has grown the feathers it needs for flight. Still the young ones return to the nest regularly where their parents continue to feed them while teaching them to hunt.

In a week or two the young storks will be able to manage without their parents' care. They will begin to get restless, gathering together in the meadows or circling up in the sky. One day, usually about August 20, they will circle and not return. Their first long journey to Africa will have begun.

Their parents stay longer, continuing to build and improve the nests. Then in September the mature storks follow the fledglings on the long migration south.

In autumn the towns where the storks have stayed seem very quiet. But one day next spring the wonderful clattering will be heard again, announcing the arrival of the first white stork to return home.

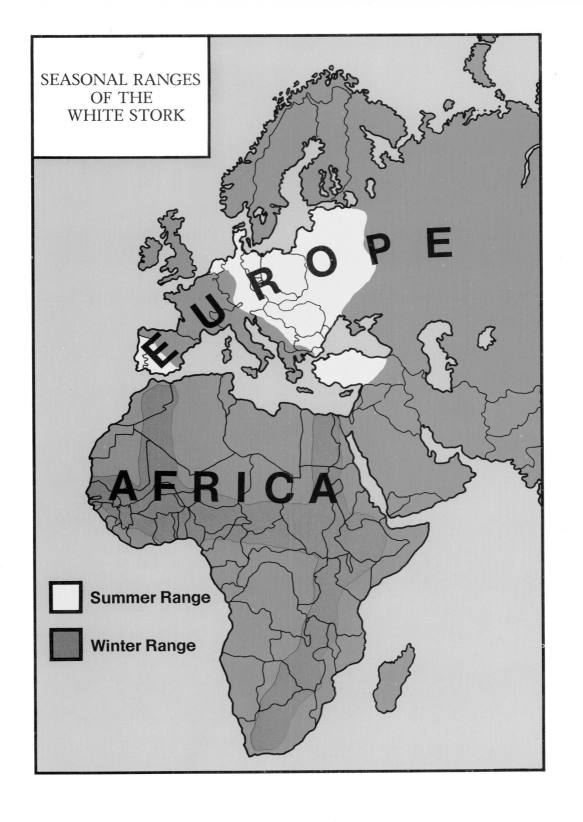

SEASONAL RANGES
OF THE
WHITE STORK

EUROPE

AFRICA

Summer Range

Winter Range

Storks are found throughout the world. Altogether, there are 17 **species**, or kinds, of storks. Just two species are found in Europe. The white stork is the most common and is the kind we have seen in this book.

All storks have partially webbed feet with four toes and leave footprints like the one pictured on the right. Their feet and long, thin legs are perfectly designed for wading on the soft, muddy bottoms of shallow streams, ponds, and lakes.

The black stork, pictured on the next page, is the other stork found in Europe. It lives only in the woodlands, is very shy, and is even rarer than the white stork.

Compared to white storks, which are under three feet tall, other stork species are quite large. Asian storks (above left) are about four feet tall or more. Some stork species found in Africa are five feet tall and have wingspans of ten feet.

The saddle-billed stork (above right) is one such large African stork. Its name comes from the yellowish "saddle" at the top of its bill.

THE WOOD STORK

The wood stork is the only stork native to the United States. It breeds and winters in the southeastern and Gulf states and sometimes strays northward in summer to South Carolina, North Carolina, and even as far as the southern tip of Illinois.

Wood storks are nearly four feet tall and have a wingspan of over five feet. They are white with black in their wings and tails. Their heads and necks are covered with dark gray scaly skin instead of feathers. Because of their bald heads, wood storks are often called "flintheads" and "gourdheads."

Wood storks gather in large colonies to breed and build their huge nests in trees. Sometimes thousands of these birds will inhabit just a small area of swampland. Usually rather silent, they will utter a low, croaking call when around their nests. Young storks, though, clatter their bills constantly.

Snakes, frogs, fish, and even young alligators are favorite foods of the wood stork. With one foot, it disturbs its prey by stirring up the marshy waters, seizes it in its bill, and then swallows it. After eating, storks often sit in treetops to rest, or they soar in circles on warm air currents.

In recent years, the number of wood storks has diminished drastically. Less than a century ago, hunters killed many storks for their feathers. People have also reduced the stork population by building on land that was previously the storks' natural habitat. Now under the protection of state and federal agencies, the wood stork should be able to flourish well into the future.

Glossary

aerie: the nest site of a white stork, usually located on the rooftop of a building

brood: When parent birds sit on their eggs or chicks to keep them warm, they are brooding.

crop: a pouch for storing food located in the necks of some birds

egg tooth: a hard pointed knob on the top of a newborn bird's bill used to break through the eggshell

extinction: When all the animals of a certain kind, or species, have died, that species is extinct.

fledgling: a young bird that has just acquired the feathers it needs for flight

fertilization: the union of a male and a female reproductive cell

incubate: to keep an egg at the proper temperature for development of the chick inside the egg

incubator: a warm, moist case used to hatch eggs

migrate: to move from one region to another, usually seasonally, for feeding or breeding. White Storks migrate between Europe and Africa.

migratory: an animal or bird that migrates. Storks are migratory birds.

preening: the cleaning of a bird's feathers. A stork preens by pulling each feather through its bill.

sperm: male reproductive cells

Index

ABOUT THE AUTHORS

Heiderose and Andreas Fischer-Nagel received degrees in biology from the University of Berlin. Their special interests include animal behavior, wildlife protection, and environmental control. The Fischer-Nagels have collaborated on several internationally successful science books for children. They attribute the success of their books to their "love of children and of our threatened environment" and believe that "children learning to respect nature today are tomorrow's protectors of nature."

The Fischer-Nagels live in Germany with their daughters, Tamarica and Cosmea Désirée.